Middle Kingdom

*This book was supported by a grant
from the Eric Mathieu King Fund of
The Academy of American Poets.*

Middle Kingdom

Poems by
Adrienne Su

Alice James Books

Library of Congress Cataloging-in-Publication Data
Su, Adrienne, 1967–
Middle Kingdom: poems / by Adrienne Su
p.   cm.
ISBN   1-882295-15-3
I. Title
PS 3569.U13M53   1997   811'.54—dc21
96-40204 CIP

Cover photograph: Courtesy of the Arthur M. Sackler
Museum, Harvard University Art Museums—The Louis
Sidney Thierry Memorial Fund and the Ernest B. and Helen
Pratt Dane Fund for the Acquisition of Oriental Art.

Cover and book design by Elizabeth Knox.

This book is set in Sabon and Papyrus.

Alice James Books are published by the Alice James Poetry
Cooperative, Inc., an affiliate of the University of Maine at
Farmington.

Alice James Books
University of Maine at Farmington
98 Main Street
Farmington, Maine 04938

2ⁿᵈ Printing
Support for this printing comes from
    The Frank M. Barnard Foundation, Inc.

Acknowledgments

Grateful acknowledgment is made to the first publishers of these poems, some in slightly different form:

Chelsea: "Claiming the Find"
Clockwatch Review: "Savannah Crabs"
Epoch (Vol. 44, No. 2): "An Afternoon in the Park"
Greensboro Review: "Four Sonnets about Food,"
    "Francine, 1949"
The Harvard Independent: "Address"
Interim: "Translation"
Massachusetts Review: "Shanghai '87"
Sojourner: "Home"
The Writer's Eye: "Under the Window"

"The Bride": Reprinted from the *Prairie Schooner* by permission of the University of Nebraska Press. Copyright 1993 by the University of Nebraska Press.

"My House in the Suburbs": Reprinted from the *Prairie Schooner* by permission of the University of Nebraska Press. Copyright 1996 by the University of Nebraska Press.

"Elegy" and "The Emperor's Second Wife" first appeared in *Aloud! Voices from the Nuyorican Poets Café*, edited by Miguel Algarín and Bob Holman, Henry Holt and Co., 1994.

The author would like to thank the Fine Arts Work Center in Provincetown, The Ralph Samuel Poetry Fellowship at Dartmouth College, and The MacDowell Colony, for their support in the writing of this book. Many thanks, also, to Darrach Dolan, Mark Doty, Laura Mullen, Pamela Renner, and Ellen Watson, for their help in shaping the manuscript. And for their invaluable lessons, much gratitude to Michael Blumenthal, Lucie Brock-Broido, Rita Dove, Seamus Heaney, Gregory Orr, and Charles Wright.

Alice James Books gratefully acknowledges support from the University of Maine at Farmington and the National Endowment for the Arts.

Contents

For Jennifer and Kendall

1

IN THE SUBURBS

Address

There are many ways of saying Chinese
in American. One means restaurant.
Others mean comprador, coolie, green army.

I've been practicing
how to walk and talk,
how to dress, what to do in a silk shop.

How to talk. America: *Meiguo,*
second tone and third.
The beautiful country.

In second grade we watched films
on King in Atlanta.
How our nation was mistaken:

They said we had hidden the Japanese
in California.
Everyone apologized to me.

But I am from Eldorado Drive
in the suburbs. Sara Lee's
pound cake thaws in the heart

of the home, the parakeet bobs on a dowel,
night doesn't move. The slumber party
teems in its spot in the dark

summer; the swimming pool gleams.
Somewhere an inherited teapot is smashed
by a baseball. There may be spaces

in the wrong parts of the face,
but America bursts with things it was never meant
to have: the intent to outlast

the centerless acres,
the wedding cake tiered to heaven.
Every season a new crop of names,

like mine. It's different
because it fits on a typewriter,
because it's first in its line,

because it is Adrienne.
It's French.
It means *artful*.

1978

Early summer. Yellow jackets hover
where an older girl makes sandwiches.
The boy with the frisbee is her lover
but we don't know it; she says she wishes

he'd leave her alone. This is one
strategy we've never played.
Other things we haven't done
include calculus, driving, moving away

from home, and crying silently all night
in rooms we paid for ourselves.
We are eleven. The sunlight
beats on our arms. When we're twelve

we'll think we know everything.
Dawn will drag at our ankles, drug
us with heat. Some far morning
one of us will wake in the snug

hold of a man she shouldn't have met,
the other trek from busy
day to night and back, and both regret
not having fucked the boy with the frisbee

because it was free. Under the evergreens
we crunch ice cubes and jeer the veins
in a mother's calves. We don't mean
to be mean, but we can't complain

about the heat all day, and we know
we'll soon be swollen and blue
and white ourselves, so now's
the time. Between the two

of us, we're twenty-two. We squint
at the volleyball game, where the sky
keeps getting in the way. Transparent
faces flit through the net and fly

toward church. Our mothers can't teach
us why; they can only give us the facts.
The time we escaped to wade in the creek
at midnight, we should never have gone back.

Hitchhikers

I've never seen one close up
before. They don't pay extra
attention to us like most
grownups. Everything about
them is covered in red dust;
their big knees press against our
backs. Our mother drives as if
she picks up people like this
regularly. "We came from
Alabama," one of them
tells us. He's skinny, and pink

from the sun; his voice is parched
and unhurried. I study
the other in the side-view
mirror. His flannel shirt is
halfway buttoned, too much sky
has bleached his hair, his pores are
huge. A light turns green and he
jerks sideways, out of my sight;
his elbow fills the mirror.
He extends an arm beside
my mother. He's holding a

pack of cigarettes. She shakes
her head; he sits back, hairy
all over, breathing slowly.
It's a long, quiet way to

Virginia-Highland. Houses
are strangely alive; their white
windows follow us like eyes.
We let the men off in front
of a diner; puffs of smoke
seem to billow out the doors
as they go. They say their thanks

and walk off. All the way home
I can smell them, feel their weight
in the back. They're probably
eating sandwiches now, and
the dirt on their fingers. Soon
they'll be gone again, to that
desert where fountains and towns
appear and sink, laughing, through
the hot sand—that red plateau
my mother once traveled to,
and back from. Where I'll go, too.

Eighteen-Year-Old Biography

1

A fat child falls in a playground.
Other kids pour sand in her mouth.

2

What distorted you into believing
boys would love you bony? Bones:
all you'll be in a hundred years.

Whoever loves you then
knew you when you were more.

3

A woman roasts a side of pig;
her daughter inhales the steam
and runs out into the snow.

But the night doesn't swallow her up.
Everywhere she goes she is still there;
the silence is as big as herself.

There is no place to go but inside.
The smell of salt and animal fat
enters each room like a man.

The Word Was My First Companion

In the flickering suburban night,
Not yet acquainted with the name of the feeling,
I did not dream, but commonly imagined

My future as a teacher or journalist,
Not thinking to address
Whether there would be a man.

My family would always speak the same language,
In no way turn alien to one another,
And there would never be a poisonous city

Where people demanded psychic space.
There would be no violations,
Only the rules. There would be no urge

To walk into an unknown cathedral & disappear.
We'd stick tight as a cocoon,
And there being more books in the world

Than I could read in a lifetime
(And no such thing as the slow
Silent robbery of that lifetime),

It would always be like this moment,
Me and the blank page, hugged by night,
Planning the grammatical future.

At Seven I Mistake a Documentary on the Internment Camps for an Announcement to All Asians in America

What will Marsy do when she wants to go roller skating?
Who will look out for Kadar, who can't bark?

Mom says Disneyland is in California. So is Hollywood.
Maybe they'll let us go, for good behavior.

The man behind the barbed wire is talking in subtitles.
He points to the white flag. He says the red spot

is the blood of the Japanese people. Everything he says
sounds like the two words I know: *arigato, sayonara.*

We'll need to know more than that. We'll have to ask
for food, and everyone will laugh at us.

My House in the Suburbs

Ten minutes in the door,
Laura's in love with each
scroll, the buddhas, our
slippers, the wood peach

in the old man's hand, my
mother's accent. From room
to room she shrieks like
a digger finding the tomb

of the terra-cotta soldiers;
she wants to know the age
of the elephant book-holder,
why the green cloisonné vase

is green. She asks *Is it
authentic?* of every painting,
candle, book. A minute
later, she's still waiting

for an answer, so I rifle
backward through the years
for rumors of empire, idle
talk of armies, engineers

of insurrection, but all
I can think of is my mother
in a blue dress and those awful
pointy glasses all mothers

wore in those days. She raises
the monkey picture to the wall
while my father appraises
the angle from the hall;

they talk in the full tones
of devotion. My mother still
makes broth from bones,
patches our pants, refills

the pantry, does not resent
anything. Years to go
before her paycheck, present-
day wardrobe, the bellows

and snarls of her overtime
evenings—No, those fights
haven't come. It's the time
of the fussy setting-right

of the framed goddess of mercy,
goldfish, donkeys, eggshells;
the kids are in no hurry
to grow up and leave, the well-

dressed living room is all
they know. Now, as Laura sighs,
the dancing lady in the tall
glass box begins to cry

the answer out, but Laura
doesn't hear it. I
look to the box, then Laura.
Of course, I hear myself reply.

Savannah Crabs

Bluish and thirsty, packed tight as oranges,
they come from the coast in the iced trunk
of the blue Buick our aunt drives. She's sunk
in thoughts of dinner and not the tinges

of dread that will stain her African violets
as she tends a back pain. She does not think
of her mother, who'll die this fall under pink
bedclothes without a goodnight; the eyelets

of her gown will spell the Chinese words
for *loneliness, lovelessness, white birds.*

When our aunt and her passengers get to town,
my brother and I crouch by the crate,
poke slow ones with sticks. Two escape;
our parents chase them with tongs around

the garden, then dump all seventy-four
in the laundry-room sink. They scuttle and flip
like fat gymnasts; they amaze us kids.
We salt them, singing *When it rains it pours.*

They spit back curses: *You'll ache; you'll smother;*
you'll never be able to talk to each other.

My aunt has brought me a spiny, off-yellow
shell, big as my hand. It sits
on the dryer, where I forget about it
to watch the steamer, where waving hello

and goodbye, the first mute batch reddens
and stills. I think of my shell and go back.
Out of it, welt-ridden legs grasp
no sand. He's ugly, a hermit, threatening.

I peer in his house and read the prophecy:
You'll find joy, but you must leave the family.

II

WOMEN AND MEN

Miss Chang Is Missing

We know it's to San Francisco
or New York—she couldn't have stopped
anywhere in between, and she requires
a coast. It's her taste for seafood
and the smell of salt water, even
industrial ocean. She couldn't

have been abducted; she would have
karate-chopped the guy's pistol,
snapped his partner's neck. She wouldn't
have run away—in spite of herself
she's the Buddha
through and through; she dissolves

ill humor with her eyes. Nor
has she eloped; she doesn't like men
as much as she likes lemongrass prawns
with black pepper, and marriage
in the only world she knows
doesn't suit her. She once talked

about relatives in Hong Kong, but
they must have perished years ago
and her Chinese was broken anyway.
Not *was*—she isn't gone for good.
She often leaves town on short notice,
just never this short. She left

a syllable on a client's machine:
way, which could have been *wei*
the Chinese telephone greeting
or the beginning of *wait,* or
way do you think you're going
as she sometimes said. It must

be tough to have an accent
in both languages. The neighbors
think she intended to come back
that night; she hadn't taken the trash
to the curb, the cat came looking
for food, and she couldn't have vanished

into thin air. But she was
oriental in a way most Asian people
aren't, somehow immaterial and bound
to outlast the trees, the house,
her body—one could get in trouble
for saying it, but anyone who met her

would agree. She was the only woman
who really was that creature hovering
at the edge of the movies: dark-haired,
dark-eyed, supernatural, ginseng-
scented, otherworldly. Likely to one day
walk off the earth and into the sky.

Visitation

The dream is hardly mine; it belongs
to a thousand women gone
to teeth, dry mums, pelvic bones

that won't burn—but it visited me
last night, with some force. In it,
the eldest son, age six, levitates

over the extended family, gathered
around the hearth. Floating
from head to head, he blesses an aunt,

a nephew, parents. An oversize bee
humming with history, he touches
each forehead with the precision

of ballet. I'm next, the eldest sister;
when he comes to me, he spits, and
hovering there, he spits again.

Why can't he let be, and move on
to the next relative? I think, then see
I must leave the house that minute;

every face is just, severe. I start
for the door. "You don't care
if I live or die," I say flatly. Later

I'll think of wittier ways to go.
All I know is out there, I'll die.
There's been some doubt

about my honor, and what matters
is not the facts but what people think
are the facts. As I lift the latch,

my mother drapes her coat over me,
her last permitted act
of nurture. I walk out the door

and into my waking life
in Provincetown at the white
height of winter, lots of land

and sea away from everyone
who brought me here.
I'm making tea and reading the life

of Oscar Wilde, who believed
in legend over fact, and paid.
Some foggy days I think I see him

walking down Commercial Street
in his cello coat, or telling off a clerk
at the A&P. I wish I could wear nice

shoes or blend in at a church retreat,
but everything I choose
to emphasize only points me up

as a freak. The hearth
scatters red ash at me.
It wants to eat. It wishes

I'd fold my true life up
into a storybook for bad kids
and feed it, nicely, to the fire.

PIRANEX

So much time and space
has gone since we made

love or like that it almost
didn't happen, and most

of the time I don't think
of you, you don't think

of me, and all's well. But
now and then I guess at what

took me off your list of friends
and exes, since we were friends

before we were exes, and you're
still on mine. You're

silent on all sides. I must
still be dangerous

if I'm banned for the one
summer we had the run

of the city and complete
freedom to create

an atmosphere of possible
devotion and did—until

you went away the first
time and lost

your place in my book. Now,
years later, we've both found

mates for life, but by your decree
we can't be friends. I guess we

retroactively broke the law
and this is jail. But I recall

clearly as television the knot
in my chest the day you got

on the plane for the rest
of the world, and you must

remember how, when you
finally came home, there wasn't room

for your stuff. We're hardly going
back there. Sweet young

face in my old life, someday
you'll be stooped and I'll be gray

and we won't laugh about the hot
season we were twenty-two. Not

a word will pass between
you and any woman

you ever kissed, except
your wife, who couldn't care less

by that stage. And I'll be
a grandmother and so will she,

and every now and then I'll
be playing Scrabble

with the kids and find I have
the letters of your name save

one. Proper nouns being
outlawed, I won't even

think of spelling it out.
Instead I'll consider how

it keeps coming back, how
some disappearances grow,

don't fade—how this particular
retreat pops up in drawers

and boxes like a long-unfinished
cross-stitch or a wish

that never worked out. The kids
will shout, "Grandma! It's

your *turn*!" to re-alert me
to the game, and I'll use my three

full minutes up, then claim
the elderly exemption from time

limits, and they'll whine.
I'll rearrange and realign

the letters, but they'll be the same
as ever: PIX_E, EXP_AIN,

EPAIR, EXPAN, each winning
word refusing and refusing and refusing

to be complete.

Antidepressant

The purple pill rattles
out of its tinted bottle,

makes my hands therefore my pen
shake, cloaks me in thirteen

layers of delusionary fur,
stunts my walk, and blurs

each stark moment so it won't
be so stark. At last I don't

know what time it is
sometimes. I like this

effect all right, although
I'm still sad. Night goes

too fast, bringing sun,
whose brash light comes

unwanted into each crevice
of the apartment. This

could be a matter of life
circumstance and pills might

be the wrong fix, but I know
things won't change if I go

to Spain or take up fencing.
I'd be the same wincing

Adrienne, only armed
or in Spain. What harm

in staying by the window
to think, wish, swallow

pellets of hope, and not eat?
I'm not unrequited, don't need

company, haven't lost friend
or family. I just tend

to be a sick plant,
and no antidepressant

can shield me from the sun's
burning; leaves drop one

by one to the sill. I'll win
my war yet. My angel isn't

dead, just lost on the moon
or snowed in, gone but soon

to come, nudged out of sight
by another sleep's night.

Men

There are those you wish for and never get, for various reasons.
There are those you don't want but accept, because they are
    persuasive.
And there are those you wish for and get,

Close in their unfamiliarity, unpredictable.
Whatever he says, whatever he orders in a restaurant,
You never know how a man is going to kiss,

And it is often worth finding out. But half the time you end up
    angry
Or the object of his humiliated rage,
And you're sorry it all happened,

Sorry for everything
Except the death-defying moment
When you broke through the wall of not-touching

And you instantly knew
Not just the sort of lover he would be
But every person he ever was:

The lean adolescent, trying new boots.
The young man, snagging a shimmering bluefish.
The living man, this minute, feeling his way through the black
    universe.

Elegy

You said the last word with your last
breath and I was not there to bury
it. You spent your life writing
the note and intended
to go alone; you knew what
to say but *poof!* you were out

of breath—the night went out,
the chills passed, the last
gesture stopped. What
took a little longer was to bury
you. Everyone thought you intended
to stay; you were writing

me letters and though I wasn't writing
back, you said you had risen out
of despair and intended
to forget the last
ten years, in which you had buried
so many skeletons you didn't know what

you were born for. Anyway. What
you didn't count on was writing
the note, dying, and no one coming to bury
you. The police didn't check out
the shed until the last
of the month; they intended

to go home by dark, then opened your untended
grave at dinnertime. What
gets me is not that I was your last
woman, nor that I was off writing
term papers when you walked yourself out
of the world, not even that they'd bury

you and not invite me, but that you buried
your body where you intended
to be found and were sniffed out
belatedly, faceless, unmanly. What-
ever threw that wrench, I'm writing
you out of my memory as fast

as I can. The last word's been buried
but it's in your handwriting. You intended
to get what you got. Now get out.

An Afternoon in the Park

Below my window, a man is being ordered
to hand over cash. In all my months in the heart
of the city, I've been lost only once, in Central Park
among the trees. I walked perplexed three quarters

of an hour, from path to bridge to other path
I didn't know, Sunday morning to Sunday
afternoon. I'd always known that someday
I'd be found, that the light, pines, grass

and I would meet here. I wasn't thinking these
thoughts, but the start of them receded when
I reached a clearing where a hundred men
were sunning. They were facing into the breeze

and didn't see me. I thought I recognized one,
then remembered where he was: he'd followed
a vision to New York, had loved, lost, and hollowed
out. He left for the South and didn't come

back. In the bright clearing I watched for a sign,
didn't get one, and slipped back into the woods.
I found Fifth Avenue in minutes but could
not sleep for weeks. Now wherever I go I find

two hundred closed eyes, grass bleached
by light, bare chests burning. Since that day
I've asked about the sun, the men, the Sunday
I got lost; I've inquired at work, school, each

home I enter, at parties, but no one tells
me. Everywhere I go I meet anxious women
with money and beautiful faces, and men
with ashes on their brows. I'm lonely as hell.

Dog Winter

for the unidentified woman found at Race Point Dunes,
Provincetown, Massachusetts, 1979, with both hands missing

Handless and ageless,
you're with us as we run
with Sadie, the pup,
under chilly sun.

Alive as none of us,
the young Lab skids
among headstones, thistle,
frozen twigs.

She loves her outings
to the graveyard, where
you're always waiting,
friend in all weather.

Like the artists who flock here,
your killer searched
for a spot where he might
be alone with his work.

What were you doing
that still day?
Were you out for a run
in the hushed shade?

Did the villain spring
out of the wood
or did you meet on the path
with a start and a "Good

afternoon"? There must
have been moments
when you thought you'd slipped
into dream, that it wasn't

true when he took
your hand. Of the four
of us here, only Sadie
can say. You're

mute, we're
deaf; the dog
tunes in to the sounds
of the dead as she trots

among stones. Tell them!
somebody calls.
Tell them! I saw!
Her name was—

Sadie hears
and understands.
Her legs move her
through fields of hands.

Teeth bared,
she chases a ball,
tugs at the leash,
making us fall,

and yips at a bird.
She does not tell us.
She's unperturbed
by the cries and smells.

She is just a dog
in a thin brown coat,
beginning her life.
Although she knows

the dead witnesses
try, she also
knows what she's meant
to do on this frozen

earth. In the cold
bed where no one
disturbs you, dreams
pass unopened;

animals steal
each night across
the face concealed
by earth and frost.

By day we visit
your brittle home
and sometimes stop
to read the stones.

Sousa. May.
The dog pulls.
We stand firm
till she finally

sits, watchful,
ready to go,
her body melting
a circle of snow.

III

DEA EX MACHINA

In Mexico City

My mother's Spanish comes back to her, *poco a poco,*
in taxicabs, in bustling markets. She doesn't know

where it's coming from; she simply conceives a meaning
and the words wrap around it as if she were eighteen

again, the one from China, enrolled in Spanish One
at a girls' college in Georgia (now they call it *women's*).

She rescues us from wrong stops of the train, translates
how much the ragged child wants for a sweating grape

soda, reads all the signs. My father, who hates vacations,
gets bored and falls asleep in a chair at the Museo

del Caracol. He was an engineer even
before he came to America and sees no reason

to ogle art. My parents met in Atlanta, among
the students who couldn't go home; although her native tongue

was Shanghai, his Fuzhou, they went on dates in Mandarin
and English, in which they married and had us, who talk in

TV-English and study Latin, on my mother's
recommendation, because it "paves the way to other

languages." Now, in the plush hotel, she says the return
of Spanish reminds her of the Portuguese she learned

as a girl one summer in Brazil, with her world-wise adoptive
parents, whose American English has moments of emphasis

in Yiddish. *Mazeltov,* my Jewish grandpa would tell me
every Chinese New Year, and *gongxi facai.* "Happy

New Year," I'd answer. One year in Japan with them,
my mother learned six forms of *pardon me* and *when's*

the last bus?, all deferential, since she was a child.
Meanwhile, my father was growing up under the mild

breezes of Fujian, China, when school was interrupted
by Japan. "Atrocities," he said, abruptly

and without elaboration, about the things he saw.
He'd made no plans to leave, but now we're one and all

American, and we're touring the Basilica
de Guadalupe, and all that afternoon I'm filled with the

rhythms and turns of Spanish, and soon begin to wish my
only foreign language weren't so dead and dry

and square. Who says *quid pro quo? id est?* Meaning
to learn all the Romance languages, I'm reading

this book *Italian Is Easy If You Know Latin;* I know
some words already from music: *arpeggio, crescendo,*

pianissimo—the worst, as I always thump a key
on the fade-out. Now, according to the Mexico-City

tour guide—and here the facts may be confused by time
or translation—we're looking at the ages-old, genuine

flesh of the Virgin Mary's arm in a little glass box.
I think of the summer camp in Georgia where I did not

go forward in chapel to let Jesus into my heart
but said to myself *I'll let him in privately, I'd rather not*

hold hands with those dumb kids and quietly, not moving
a muscle, decided I had admitted him—though proving

it could be difficult. After that, I often wondered
if it worked if you didn't do anything, or speak—wondered,

in fact, if he existed. So here I am, in church
again, with proof of the flesh and a flash of faith, when they herd

us out alongside bosomy grandmothers from Tupelo.
That night we feast again on the devalued *peso:*

My father orders a monkey's brain; my brother and I are
grossed out. While we gag and cringe and exaggerate, our

parents discuss matters in Mandarin. Eventually
I, too, will learn Chinese properly, sit in the chilly

language lab in Harvard's Boylston Hall, chanting
yi, er, san, si, wu, liu, qi—thrilling my family

until I give up three years later and take Japanese
instead. Japanese doesn't threaten me. Knowing Chinese

somehow erases my right to be me; it causes cashiers
and dental hygienists to rave about my English. My dear

friend Anne, who's Japanese-American, has the same
trouble with *Nihongo*. After class we complain:

They think we were born knowing *kanji*. Grubby students
    of classical
Japanese call her up and speak it. *The assholes,*

she says, *why can't they just say, "Hi, Anne, do you want to go
out for dinner?"* But let's get back to Mexico:

My mother and I are out walking when we hear
a whistle, the same in every country; a man leers

out the window of a passing car. A truck
slows down at us. My mother tells the driver to *fuck*

off in Spanish; she doesn't know how on earth she knows
the words. Surprised, she laughs out loud. She would never
    have said those

things in English in the days she was in school.
But it works; the truck driver's astounded by the cool

composure of this extra-petite, foreign, Chinese-
looking woman with a Chinese-Japanese-Portuguese-

Jewish-American accent. He disappears. All the way
back to the hotel, we go obscured by her oddly

autonomous vocabulary. If I chose,
I could talk with equal verve; for once I know

I could say bad words, yell them in fact, and not be told
Watch your language. But strangely, I can't—I'm not old

enough or quick, or now that I'm allowed, I don't want to.
All I know is I don't know. There are so many words to

be learned, and it seems my mother knows them all. Equally
fearless in all countries, she is absolutely

articulate. And I'm speechless. As she enters the room
where my father has the television tuned

to American football, she's somehow beyond irritation. Her face
is a girl's. Meanwhile, my brother has emptied my green suitcase

onto the floor in search of his lost Hershey's with Almonds.
I open my mouth to yell—but stop when I sense a calming,

unearthly presence I cannot describe hovering over
me. It's Mary's saved arm, resting on my shoulder,

lightweight and invisible, comforting, sisterly, somewhat
maternal. I'm miles above the sinking city, way up

over the smog and the art and the chapels and the slimy
truck drivers, when my *dea ex machina* whispers to me

in easy, beautiful Latin: *Someday you'll know what to say.*
The words will come slowly, but they'll never go away.

Illumination

It happened in a green courtyard in Virginia.
It was summer and I was sixteen.
Some kids I knew walked by and waved,
and I waved back, unable to move.

The moment held me there.
I felt unobtrusive for the first time
and knew that if things had happened differently,
I could disappear among them,

but—also for the first time—I had a purpose.
At once it lifted me off the concrete path
and anchored me to the ground.
                              This was to be my life.

I could go to them, but now, knowing I could,
would not. I would stand in the hot doorway
just out of the sun, and watch the light pass over the brow
of the boy I wanted to walk with,

and tell of his face and shoulders, the damp air, and the
    desire for him.

Translation

I was born in summer
with a small black stone

planted inside my chest
like a spot on the lungs.

Every year it grows harder
to breathe, the air toxic

as the river I enter
not expecting to drown.

I'm a talking lie
made of bones

and ideas. A myth without
an archetype. I go from city

to city proclaiming
about life, when what I know

is words
not things

IV

MIDDLE KINGDOMS

Under the Window

Day and night in the green hospital,
the woman whose name means Fortunate Jade
grows smaller. Her son forgets

more Chinese with every visit.
He sits by the bed and cries tearlessly.
He is fifteen and remembers his birthplace

as the sputter of its two taxis,
chickens in a wire box, deep-fried
oysters, and guttural speech.

Even in health, his mother looked
small in the supermarket aisles.

She hated the food; she said the people
were dumb as animals. For the last

year, her flesh has been slowly
making its way back to China.

Her son does not tell her
she is still beautiful
even though he knows the words.

He rearranges the camellias,
asks her if she wants TV.
He jumps up, sits down, changes

the water in her glass. He is in love
for the first time and can't talk
about it in any language.

This is the boy she prayed for,
implored all the gods,
even the foreign one, to deliver.

He arrived with a clear cry,
the first son of his generation.
The house filled with blessings

and fat red envelopes. Her husband
found work in America, where
they learned to drive cars—

and now this. Perhaps it was ill luck,
a bad ancestor, the nameless daughter
she had prayed out of existence.

It could be the water
from the strange pipes
or the foul teas she'd sipped

to turn the not-yet child
into a boy. It could be
the songs she had crooned

to her belly, not thinking
of the unblessed rice paddies,
the slighted earth, the moon

that now glared into her window
through each night, saying
You will not sleep. You will not sleep.

Francine, 1949

Then there was a revolution.

The underpopulated street
would have to do, its mulberries
abnormally large, the moon too high.

She would plant basil and wait.
The people were not strange,
did not live by the wrong clock,

no, it was the impenetrable soil
and their blindness
to its refusals.

Each long day
ended over the hills
while they conversed at tables,

no wonder,
no resignation,

just the incessant motion,
the not-digging.

She had plenty
to worry about: nieces
in the neighborhood,

her sisters back home.
She would teach the girls
to keep silkworms;

she'd stand in the window
as her mother had, in another place,
watching peddlers and strays.

Against the enormous landscape
she would pickle and knit
like a pioneer wife, and one day

return to her sisters,
not all of them mothers
but all of them matronly

in shawls identical to hers
but muted, each child departed
for a new language,

the house demolished,
two new graves on the hill.
At least the mountains

would not have moved,
the one with the frog-lip
still frog-lipped,

the ones whose tops
vanished into the sky
vanished into the sky.

The Emperor's Second Wife

I light the extra room and stay there nights
when I'm not called. I curl in the empty quilt
and know she's with him. I pull the blankets tight

and hope I won't remember how she goes
to him in nothing, original and dank, denying
little. She understands his need; she knows

I'm filling in the nights when she's unwilling.
She knows I'm twelve years old and only starting.
But I'm the one whose sleep is shallow, spilling

into day. He's everything to me but lover.
He tells me, if we don't make love, it's right.
It's best my spirit stay intact, all over.

No one else must know. They think the two
of us are fucking all the time we're here.
But we just talk. The rustling girls who do

my nails are scared for me. They think I'll swell
before the winter. But in the chamber's privacy
he only wants to hold me, kiss me, touch, and tell

me I am gracious. He won't do violation
— that's how he calls it—so we lie beside
each other, tumid with desire and the patience

of two statues. *It's wrong,* he says. *You're young.*
You should be learning grammar. I cover my face
when he says these things. I ache. I've just begun

to see the error. He thinks girls happen slower,
that as long as we're unopened, we're immune
to breaking. He imagines I'm intact all over.

That lady must go. When I learn magic,
I'll erase her, have her put away for stealing.
But she doesn't hate me back. She brings elastic

ribbons, ties my hair in twists. She comes
with plates and pastries. She gives me stockings,
pins, and slips, and asks me if our husband's won

me over. I tell her he is all a girl
could want, and more. She snickers when I say it,
then agrees. In recent months our emperor's revealed

another side. He can't be still. She likes
my work. It's clear she thinks I do the service.
We talk about his mouth, his hands, his eyes

and feet. She says, when I'm a few years older
I'll be deadly. She thinks I never cry,
that I'm serene, divine, immune. Intact, all over.

The Bride

*Note: In a small town in southern China, the people once believed
that the first man to sleep with a woman would be fatally poisoned
by the act, but if a woman remained a virgin all her life, she would
die by the same poison. Shortly before a wedding, the bride's family
hired someone from another town to remove the curse.*

I will marry tomorrow, purified.
My father chose you to do it
because you are from other parts,
dispensable and willing.

The man my mother took
turned ninety before he was thirty.
His teeth yellowed
and the coins went with him in a cave
down south.

I am twenty years old.
I carry this toxin like a baby.
If you do not have me, it will.
Welts will rise and my throat will inflame.
I will strangle my sister's child, go blind,
drown myself in a well.

You think I am already a crazy girl
with crazy parents, in the town
where they worship the wrong gods.
Silver from my grandmother waits for the taking.

When I was a girl I worried
that I would perish an unwilling suicide,
but here you are. Now that I have seen your face
it will hover like a birdsong, every morning.

Even though the man left no child,
I ask my mother how she lives with his image.
She says it is her only murder,
but necessary.

Already I think I know you,
not as one of us
but as a foreigner with strange vision
and a mad desire, because I give dying
and you are about to take it, like food.

Your home is only a week away on foot,
but you barely speak our dialect.
Your shoulders are wide and you don't laugh.
You are all body, a New Year's pig,
ghostless, bought for me by my father.

That is already all I can think about:
the deadly thing
and how you will end up dust.

Tomorrow I will put on the red dress.
I thought it would be different, venomlessness.
It will be good to be a mother, a maker
of dye and candles, a hoarder
of coins and blankets, coats.

Claiming the Find

I woke when last light seeped
across the ceiling, the start
of evening and the neat
gathering of plates happening

all over town. The overheard
sojourners next door
murmured until I stirred
to find a wall, a floor,

the same lace bedspread
everyone turned at night,
the ubiquitous red Thermos
and a bowl enameled white.

All day I'd lolled
in the sleeper with books,
curled, leaned toward the glass
for light, or a look

at houses squatting
in long grey rows, patched gowns
swinging from rods, rotting
domestic fruit. In these towns

I recognized the same hats,
roadside cooks, the upright
walls of empire. The elusive fact
of arrival had teased me last night

when I sloughed into a squealing
rickshaw, held out an address,
huddled inside, almost kneeling
in the cart. The rain pressed

down, marbles from the sky.
I clutched the scrawled house number
like a talisman, then knew why
the destination hovered

like a Chinese Oz. That plain
washbowl waited like a favorite dog
in each cold hall. I could explain
presence as we bumped and slogged

ahead: sprinkling brown
bread crumbs instead of stones,
stumbling on a foreign town
where the water tastes like home.

Shanghai '87

I follow a man and a thin woman up the stairs
of my mother's house. They are the first-floor family.
From a door on the second, a diminished woman
in a cotton gown watches. Hers is the room
my aunts slept in before they joined the traffic
racing south, before the country shook its unbearable

holders. The house faces the road. Now an unbearable
clamor of bells and horns confuses the upstairs
muttering of women who no longer hear the traffic
hauling. Since the revolution, no family
member has reclaimed the house, twelve rooms
and a balcony. I'm a fresh intruder, a woman

who looks Chinese and claims to be child of a woman
named Chang. But my pronunciation is unbearable;
I was raised in the land of milk. Here is the room
my mother shared with brothers. We climb another stair
and I start to think in Chinese. All the family
to come will be born in English. Once, the traffic

of servants congested the landings; now the traffic
is of neighbors. From an oak-framed mirror, a woman
with my grandmother's face considers me. Her family
is about to disperse, the sons to travel unbearable
distances east. Her husband will descend the stairs
to a war. Now, in the master bedroom,

two children are directing toy trucks. The room
fills with Chinese sound effects and the traffic
of miniature pickups. From the upstairs
balcony, I can see a diving pool; a woman
or a man does laps. Through my first ten unbearable
Georgian summers, my mother took the family

swimming twice a week. She was ten when her family
left everything, the dogs, the domestics, the rooms
and banisters. In '66 a great aunt wrote of unbearable
climate. She did not mean heat. The clattering traffic
pauses and resumes. When I follow the thin woman
and her husband down the stairs,

the stairs complain. No one is left of the family.
All we have, the woman is saying, *is the first-floor room.*
Shanghai is crowded as Tokyo. The traffic is unbearable.

China

You are all strange and what am I doing
without a plan?

Nothing along the train tracks.
Too much sugar in the lotus-root pudding—

My personal Narnia
is not personal at all.

After dinner we slurp noodles
and a boiled egg

so everyone will live forever
like the shining idea

of the other land, blessed
by the one good spirit

whose breath
rustles the fine crop—

like the people everywhere wishing,
as they enter sleep,

to sway in those long fields
far away, without season.

Four Sonnets about Food

I

Words can't do
what bird bones
can: stew
to the stony
essence
of one
small soul, the spent
sacrifice boiled down
to the hard white
matter that nourishes
the mighty
predator, who flourishes
on the slaughtered
animal and water.

2

Who feeds
another is like bones
to him who eats
(I say "him" only
because it is a man
in my house
who eats and a woman
who goes about
the matter of sustenance),
food being always
a matter of life and
death and each day's
dining
another small dying.

3

Scallops seared
in hot iron
with grated ginger,
rice wine,
and a little oil
of sesame, served
with boiled
jasmine rice, cures
the malaise
of long, fluorescent
weekdays
spent
in the city
for money.

4

I am afraid
I can't always be
here when you need
a warm body
or words; someday
I'll slip
into the red clay
I started with
and forget
who you are,
but
for now, here's
my offering: baked red
fish, clear soup, bread.

Home

It is a long way back,
more than a drive
from dawn to the black
hours. It is five

thousand days to a sky-blue
summer of swelling
and pain, in which two
sisters stopped telling

their secrets. It means
restoring a dead man
to his office to dream
and tally, and a woman

to a classroom full
of girls, whom she orders
into the hall
and orders

to stop crying.
It's not just that,
either; a dying
uncle must come back

to his bed in the city,
Chinese be forgotten,
and four pretty
faces erased. Often

I wake under the high
ceiling and can't
remember why
I'm here, and want

to die. Then years
of memory revive
noisily, in clear
focus, but my life

isn't mine. One
of the girls in the hall
has stopped and undone
her hair, which falls

generously down
her back all the way
to the floor. Her round
shoulders are bare. A

moment later, so is
her back. Her legs
are bare. She is
laughing, and the next

instant there's no girl
to speak of,
just the door and the hall
she's walked out of.

Recent Titles from Alice James Books

Doug Anderson, *The Moon Reflected Fire*
Robert Cording, *Heavy Grace*
Deborah DeNicola, *Where Divinity Begins*
Theodore Deppe, *The Wanderer King*
Rita Gabis, *The Wild Field*
Kinereth Gensler, *Journey Fruit*
Forrest Hamer, *Call and Response*
Cynthia Huntington, *We Have Gone to the Beach*
Sharon Kraus, *Generation*
E. J. Miller Laino, *Girl Hurt*
Richard McCann, *Ghost Letters*
Nora Mitchell, *Proofreading the Histories*
Carol Potter, *Upside Down in the Dark*
Ellen Watson, *We Live in Bodies*

Alice James Books has been publishing poetry since 1973. One of the few presses in the country that is run collectively, the cooperative selects manuscripts for publication through competitions. New authors become active members of the press, participating in editorial and production activities. The press, which places an emphasis on publishing women poets, was named for Alice James, sister of William and Henry, whose gift for writing was ignored and whose fine journal did not appear in print until after her death.